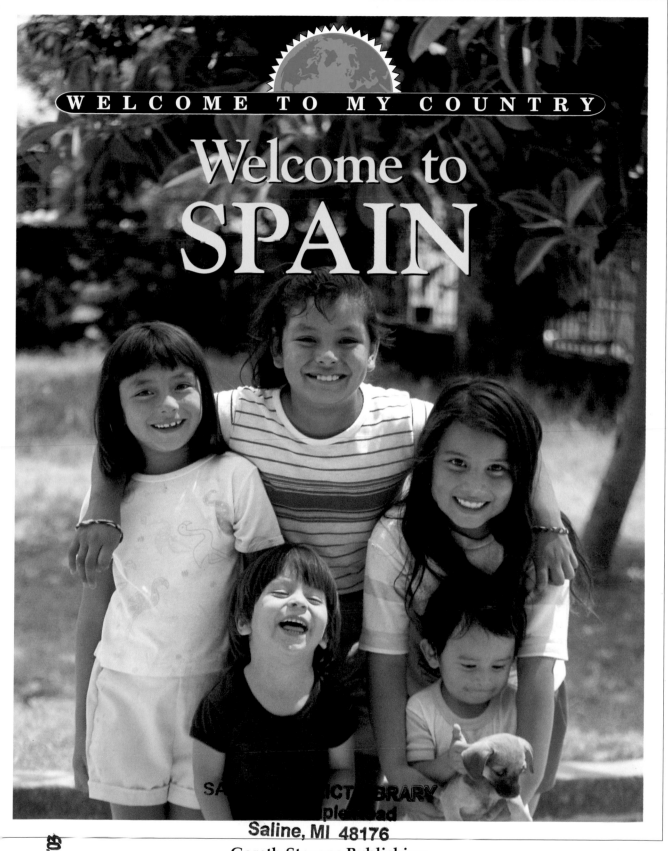

WELCOME TO MY COUNTRY

Welcome to
SPAIN

Gareth Stevens Publishing
A WORLD ALMANAC EDUCATION GROUP COMPANY

Written by
GERALDINE MESENAS/KATHERINE GRINSTED

Designed by
HASNAH MOHD ESA

Picture research by
SUSAN JANE MANUEL

First published in North America in 2000 by
Gareth Stevens Publishing
A World Almanac Education Group Company
1555 North RiverCenter Drive, Suite 201
Milwaukee, Wisconsin 53212 USA

For a free color catalog describing
Gareth Stevens' list of high-quality books
and multimedia programs, call
1-800-542-2595 (USA) or
1-800-461-9120 (CANADA).
Gareth Stevens Publishing's
Fax: (414) 225-0377.

© **TIMES MEDIA PRIVATE LIMITED 2000**
Originated and designed by
Times Editions
an imprint of Times Media Private Limited
Times Centre, 1 New Industrial Road
Singapore 536196
http://www.timesone.com.sg/te

Library of Congress Cataloging-in-Publication Data

Mesenas, Geraldine.
Welcome to Spain / Geraldine Mesenas and Katherine Grinsted.
p. cm. — (Welcome to my country)
Includes bibliographical references and index.
Summary: An overview of the geography, history, government,
economy, people, and culture of Spain.
ISBN 0-8368-2512-8 (lib. bdg.)
1. Spain—Juvenile literature. [1. Spain.] I. Title. II. Series.
DP17.M55   2000
946—dc21   00-020789

Printed in Malaysia

1 2 3 4 5 6 7 8 9 04 03 02 01 00

PICTURE CREDITS
Bes Stock: 45
Camera Press: 14 (top), 15 (top), 37 (top)
Focus Team — Italy: 2, 5, 31 (top), 36
Haga Library Inc., Japan: Cover, 3 (center),
    4, 18, 27 (bottom), 38
HBL Network Photo Agency: 3 (bottom), 6,
    8, 10, 14 (bottom), 19, 26, 27 (top), 30,
    32, 33, 39, 40, 41
Illustrated London News Picture Library:
    15 (bottom)
North Wind Picture Archives: 11, 12, 15
    (center), 29
Christine Osborne: 16, 31 (bottom)
Chip and Rosa Maria de la Cueva Peterson:
    7, 20, 25, 28
David Simson: 3 (top), 17, 22, 23, 24, 34,
    35, 37 (bottom)
Still Pictures: 9 (both)
Tan Chung Lee: 1
Topham Picturepoint: 13
Travel Ink: 43
Trip Photographic Library: 21

Digital Scanning by Superskill Graphics Pte Ltd

Contents

Words that appear in the glossary are printed in **boldface** type the first time they occur in the text.

4

Welcome to Spain!

Spain is famous for its beautiful beaches and mountains. The Strait of Gibraltar separates Spain from Africa. Many years ago, the Spanish Empire ruled over most parts of the world. Today, Spain is home to people of various ethnic groups. Let's learn about the history and culture of the Spaniards.

Opposite: The church of the Sagrada Família was designed by Antonio Gaudí, one of Spain's most famous architects.

Below: Spaniards love to sing and dance at *ferias* (feh-REE-uhs), where people buy and sell horses and bulls.

The Flag of Spain

The Spanish flag has two red bands separated by a yellow band. The shield in the center of the flag is a combination of the **coats of arms** of the former kingdoms of León, Castile, Navarra, and Aragón.

The Land

Spain is the third largest country in Europe. Sandy beaches dominate the eastern coast of Spain, which faces the Mediterranean Sea. In contrast, the northern coast of Spain, which meets the Atlantic Ocean, is rocky and rugged. The Spanish territory includes the Canary Islands, the Balearic Islands, and the cities of Ceuta and Melilla on the Moroccan coast.

Below: The Pyrenees mountain range is a natural border between France and Spain. It protected early Spain from European invaders.

Spain is a mountainous country. Its tallest peak is Pico de Teide, which is located on the island of Tenerife. It stands at 12,198 feet (3,718 meters). The Pyrenees mountain range forms a natural border with France in the north.

The harsh and dry Meseta, one of the largest plateaus in Europe, sits in the center of the country. Fertile plains are found near the coasts. Spain's longest river is the Ebro.

Above: The Strait of Gibraltar in southern Spain separates the country from the African continent. It also connects the Atlantic Ocean and the Mediterranean Sea.

Climate

The Cantabrian Mountains separate two regions of Spain that have distinctly different climates. To the north of this range lies "green Spain," which has mild winters and cool summers. "Dry Spain" lies to the south of the range. This region has bitter winters and dry summers, with little rainfall throughout the year.

The Mediterranean coast has a subtropical climate, with hot summers and wet winters.

Above: A range of landscapes is found in Andalusia, in southern Spain. In this region, fertile plains give way to dry, desert land nearer the coast.

Plants and Animals

Many species of plants and animals can be found in Spain. Vast forests cover the mountain slopes. Spain's most common agricultural products include cork, oak, olives, and grapes. Southeastern Spain is mainly desert.

Rabbits and partridge are commonly found in Spain, while wolves, wildcats, and deer are rarer. An abundance of aquatic life thrives in the Atlantic Ocean and the Mediterranean Sea.

Above and below: Spain's national parks provide homes for many rare animals, such as the European wolf (*above*) and griffon vultures (*below*).

History

Early Settlers

Many different groups of people settled in Spain over its long history. Between 800 and 500 B.C., the Phoenicians from the Middle East, the Greeks, the Iberians from North Africa, and the Celts from northern Europe all established communities in Spain.

The Catholic faith became the official state religion when a Germanic tribe, called the Visigoths, invaded Spain in the fifth century A.D.

Left: The **Moors**, who ruled Spain for many centuries, built the Alhambra. It is a remarkable palace with lovely gardens and intricate stonework.

Left: In 1492, Italian explorer Christopher Columbus set sail for the New World, with the support of Queen Isabella and King Ferdinand of Spain.

The Moors and the New World

The Moors, who were Muslims from North Africa, invaded most of Spain in 711. During their rule, trade flourished, along with the arts and sciences.

In 1469, Isabella I of Castile married Ferdinand II of Aragón, joining their two powerful kingdoms. In 1492, the Spanish army reclaimed Spain from the Moors, and the conquest of the **New World** began.

The Spanish Empire

In the 1500s, the Spanish Empire included a large portion of the New World and Europe. Spanish culture flourished. Queen Isabella's and King Ferdinand's grandson, Charles I, became the most powerful ruler in Europe.

The Spanish Empire started to decline in 1588, when the English navy defeated the Spanish fleet of ships, called the Armada. By 1898, Spain lost its American colonies and other territories in Asia and South America.

Below: The Catholic monarchs, Isabella and Ferdinand, ordered the Spanish Inquisition, which imprisoned and killed people who did not strictly follow the Catholic faith.

Left: Many countries were involved in the Spanish Civil War. Germany and Italy supported the Nationalists, while the Soviet Union, France, and Mexico supported the Republicans.

The Spanish Civil War

In the early 1900s, Spain was plagued by political problems. In 1936, the Spanish Civil War broke out between the Republicans and the Nationalists (the army). After nearly three years of fighting, the military took over Madrid on March 28, 1939. On April 1, military leader General Francisco Franco declared himself chief of state.

From Franco to Modern Times

General Franco ruled Spain under a **military dictatorship**, which took away the people's freedom. He relaxed his rule during the 1950s and 1960s, however, and the economy flourished.

Franco died in 1975, and Juan Carlos became the king of Spain. In 1978, a **parliamentary monarchy** was established. The people approved a new constitution, which recognized that Spain consists of many regions, with people of many nationalities and languages. Since 1996, the Popular Party has headed the government.

Above: When Juan Carlos became king of Spain on November 22, 1975, he promised to restore **democracy** in Spain.

Left: The royal palace was built in the eighteenth century. Situated in Madrid, the palace is used for state occasions.

Queen Isabella I (1451–1504)

The queen of Castile, Isabella I sponsored Christopher Columbus's voyage to the New World. She greatly supported the Catholic Church and banned all other religions in Spain.

Isabella I

Charles I (1500–1558)
(Holy Roman Emperor Charles V)

The grandson of Isabella and Ferdinand, Charles became king of Spain when he was seventeen years old. During his reign, the Spanish Empire included much of Europe and the Americas.

Charles I

General Francisco Franco (1892–1975)

General Francisco Franco governed Spain from 1939 to 1975. The country **stabilized** during Franco's reign, but his rule was very strict, and many people were executed.

Francisco Franco

Government and the Economy

Government

In Spain's parliamentary monarchy, established in 1978, the king is the official head of state. Real power, however, lies with the prime minister, who is the head of government and is elected by the people.

Below: The parliament is made up of two houses, one of which is the Congreso de los Diputados, or the Congress of Deputies, located in the capital, Madrid.

The parliament consists of two houses — the Congress of Deputies and the Senate. Members of both houses serve four-year terms.

Spain is divided into seventeen regions, with a total of fifty provinces within them. Each province has an elected council and a governor.

The judicial system in Spain is headed by the General Council of Judicial Power.

Men between twenty-one and thirty-five years of age are required to serve a certain length of time in the military.

Above: The two most powerful political parties in Spain are the Spanish Socialist Workers' Party (PSOE) and the Popular Party.

Agriculture

Agriculture, or farming, along with forestry and fishing, are important parts of the Spanish economy. Because the Spanish climate is very dry, the main crops are grapes, olives, and wheat, which do not require much water. The government provides water for other crops through **irrigation**. Spain exports a large portion of its produce to western Europe.

Above: Farmers harvest olives in winter to make olive oil or to pickle in brine. Many olive orchards are located in Andalusia in southern Spain.

Industry and Tourism

Industrial growth in Spain began in the mid-1950s. Today, the most important goods manufactured in Spain include cloth, motor vehicles, ships, iron, and steel. The country's main trading partners are Japan, the United States, and several European countries.

Another important industry in Spain is tourism. Each year, more than 65 million tourists flock to Spain's beaches, coastal resort towns, and historical sites.

Below: Barcelona, on the eastern coast of Spain, is one of the busiest ports in the Mediterranean.

People and Lifestyle

Over the centuries, many groups of people have settled in Spain, including the Phoenicians, Romans, Visigoths, and Moors. Today, 39.4 million people live in Spain.

In the twentieth century, many people moved from rural areas to cities, such as Madrid, to look for work. Most people live in coastal areas, such as Valencia.

Above: These boys are from Toledo, a city located in central Spain.

The Importance of Family

Family is very important to the Spanish. Small, two-children families are the norm in modern Spain, but extended family ties are still valued. Grandparents, aunts, and cousins often live in the same house or nearby.

Left: A favorite Spanish pastime is an evening stroll.

Life in the City

The two largest cities in Spain, Madrid and Barcelona, are very crowded. They house one-fourth of the country's total population. Many people live in apartments outside the city center.

Ever-increasing populations in the cities have led to many problems, such as pollution and traffic congestion. Unemployment, homelessness, and crime have also increased.

Below: After a long day of school or work, people like to walk, shop, or rest on park benches.

Countryside and Rest

People in rural areas lead a traditional way of life. They live in clay or stone houses. Many farms in northern Spain are small, family-run operations, while those in southern Spain are larger.

In the past, the Spanish people went home in the afternoon for their main meal and a nap, or **siesta**. They then returned to work until late in the evening. Today, the government is trying to establish a continuous eight-hour day.

Above: Small farms dot the region of Galicia. Galicians originated from the Celtic people and speak a language called **Gallego** (guy-YAY-goh).

Education

Children between the ages of six and fourteen are required to attend school. Between the ages of six and twelve, children attend primary school. Secondary education is for children aged twelve to sixteen.

After completing secondary education, students can take either a **vocational** training course or a two-year diploma course. After this, they can take a one-year course to qualify for entrance to a university.

Left: One of Europe's oldest universities is Salamanca University in Spain. It was founded in the thirteenth century.

University students get a basic degree after three years and a higher degree after two or three more years. Economics, medicine, and law are the most popular courses of study. The main universities in Spain are located in Madrid and Barcelona.

Religion

More than 94 percent of the total Spanish population is Roman Catholic. With over sixty thousand Catholic churches, monasteries, and convents in Spain, Catholicism has played a significant role in Spanish history.

Below: Many Catholics take part in **pilgrimages**, such as this one held at the shrine of the Virgin of El Rocío in Andalusia.

Its influence can still be seen in Spanish art and literature. Religious festivals, such as Easter and Christmas, are large, **communal** affairs, as are traditional Catholic rituals, such as baptisms, marriages, and funerals.

Other Christian groups exist, the largest of which belong to the Protestant and the Eastern Orthodox churches. Jews form the largest religious group outside of Christianity. Muslims also make up a small percentage of the population in Spain.

Above: Holy Week is one of the most important events for Catholics in Spain. In the solemn procession, hundreds of people walk through the streets wearing hoods and robes. Some carry large wooden crosses.

Left: Corpus Christi is a religious festival that celebrates the triumph of good over evil. The highlight is a procession through streets covered with flowers and herbs.

Language

The Spanish language has its origins in the dialect of Castile, a powerful kingdom in the fifteenth century. Castilian became the official language of Spain in 1714.

Above: Gestures add liveliness to many conversations.

The Spanish language has been influenced by many foreign tongues, including Latin, Greek, Basque, and Celtic. Many different groups of immigrants, from countries such as Germany, France, and the Middle East, introduced new words into the Spanish language.

Spanish Literature

Much of Spanish literature is religious, and many stories tell about the struggle between Christians and Moors. The most famous Spanish literary work is the novel *Don Quixote* by Miguel de Cervantes. Many Spanish writers have won the Nobel Prize in Literature.

Opposite: *Don Quixote*, by Miguel de Cervantes, is a story about the adventures of Don Quixote and his servant, Sancho Panza, as they travel the country fighting injustice.

Arts

Spanish Architecture

Spanish architecture shows the influence of the various civilizations that have settled in the country, such as the Moors, the Celts, the French, and the North Africans. The most famous building in Spain is the Alhambra, a magnificent palace built by the Moors. One of the most renowned Spanish architects is Antonio Gaudí.

Below: The Alhambra, a stunning example of Moorish architecture, is a major tourist attraction in Spain.

Great Artists

Three of the greatest artists in Spain before the twentieth century were El Greco (1541–1614), Diego Velázquez (1599–1660), and Francisco de Goya (1746–1828).

In the twentieth century, Spanish artists, such as Pablo Picasso, Joan Miró, and Salvador Dalí, created their own unique styles and strongly influenced the art world. Picasso, one of the greatest artists of the twentieth century, founded the **cubist** movement and created over twenty thousand paintings and sculptures.

Music and Dance

Spanish musicians and composers are world famous. Some of the best opera singers, such as Plácido Domingo and José Carreras, are Spanish. Manuel de Falla, whose specialty is folk music, is one of the most renowned composers in Spain.

Well-known Spanish dances include the flamenco, the fandango, and the bolero. The most famous of these is

Above: The Salvador Dalí Museum, with its distinctive architecture, is located in Figueras, Catalonia, where Dalí was born.

the flamenco. Traditionally danced by the Gypsies of Andalusia, the flamenco is characterized by graceful hand movements and complex footwork. Guitarists accompany the dancers.

Left: In the flamenco, music and rhythm are created by hand-clapping, singers, guitarists, and **castanets**.

Leisure

Spaniards enjoy leisure time. Many meet friends at cafés after work to chat and relax. During the weekends, families have picnics in the parks or visit relatives in the countryside. On Sunday afternoons, people go to the

theaters to watch concerts or operas. Traditionally, families enjoy taking an evening stroll before dinner. In the evening, many Spaniards watch their favorite television programs.

Soccer Mania

Soccer was introduced in Spain in 1873 by English and Scottish miners, and the first club was formed in 1880. Today, soccer is the country's most popular sport. On Sundays, more than 100,000 fans fill the stadiums for regional or international matches.

Spanish teams, such as Real Madrid and FC Barcelona, are among the best in Europe. The Spanish national team is one of the best in the world, qualifying for the World Cup finals nine times.

Above: Although the national soccer team was in decline during the Spanish Civil War and World War II, it has since risen to become a very strong team.

Sports

Many world champion athletes are Spanish. One of Spain's best-loved sportsmen, Severiano Ballesteros, made golf history when he turned professional at seventeen. In tennis, Arantxa Sánchez Vicario won the 1989 French Open when she was just seventeen years old. Miguel Indurain won the Tour de France, a rigorous cycling competition, every year from 1991 to 1995.

Below: Water sports, such as sailing, wind surfing, and water skiing, are very popular in Spain.

Left: Tennis champion Arantxa Sánchez Vicario has won four Grand Slam singles titles. She earned medals at the 1996 Olympic Games.

Bullfighting

After soccer, bullfighting is the second most popular Spanish sport. The main bullrings are in Madrid and Seville. The tradition of bullfighting began as a test of men's bravery. Bullfighters, or matadors, have to exhibit not only bravery, but also agility and artistry, as they try to avoid the bull's horns. Bulls are very aggressive animals.

Today, many people think bullfighting is cruel because the bulls are killed at the end of the fight.

Below: Many Spaniards see bullfighters as both athletes and artists.

Festivals

Many of the important festivals in Spain are religious. One of the major events in the Spanish calendar is Holy Week, or Semana Santa. Processions are held throughout Spain to commemorate the death and resurrection of Jesus Christ. Another significant religious festival is Corpus Christi, which is held in May.

Christmas is celebrated on December 25, followed by the Feast of the Three Kings on January 6.

Below: The highlight of the Seville Spring Fair, held at Easter, is a horseback parade.

In February, before the beginning of **Lent**, carnivals are held all over Spain, with colorful parades and bright costumes.

In May, large groups of people make pilgrimages to the Hermitage of the Virgin of the Rocío in Almonte. Many travel on horseback or in beautifully decorated carts. During the procession, there is music, dancing, and feasting.

Above: La Tomatina is a giant tomato fight held in Buñol, Valencia, every year. In this fiesta, participants throw thousands of tomatoes at each other, and everyone is drenched in tomato juice!

Food

Left: Cooked in a shallow pan, paella may include ingredients such as tomatoes, peppers, beans, seafood, pork, and chicken.

Regional Favorites

Each region in Spain specializes in certain dishes. Northern Spain is known for its delicious seafood dishes. Asturias is famous for *fabada* (fah-BAH-dah), a stew with beans and sausage. Catalonians make delicious casseroles. Valencia and its surrounding areas are renowned for their unique rice dishes, the best known of which is *paella* (pie-AY-yah). Central Spain specializes in roast meats. Andalusians make mouthwatering fried fish.

Thirst Quenchers and Snacks

Spaniards enjoy refreshing fruit and vegetables to keep cool in the warm climate. On especially hot days, the Spanish people drink *sangría* (sang-GREE-ya), a mixture of ice, fruit, red wine, and water.

For snacking, Spaniards enjoy *tapas* (TAH-pahs), which are plates of cheese, sausage, olives, artichokes, and, sometimes, snails in garlic!

Below: Spanish children enjoy eating **churros** (CHEW-ros), which are sugared strips of fried dough.

SPAIN

N

	A	B	C	D

1

FRANCE

• Bordeaux

Guernica

• Bayonne

Gijón •

ASTURIAS

CANTABRIA

BASQUE
COUNTRY

Pamplona •

ANDORRA

GALICIA

NAVARRA

• Figueras

CANTABRIAN MTS

PYRENEES

LA RIOJA

ATLANTIC OCEAN

CASTILE-LEÓN

Duero

Saragossa •

CATALONIA

Costa Brava

2

Ebro

IBERIAN MOUNTAINS

ARAGÓN

• Barcelona

Salamanca •

MADRID ■ • Guadalajara

BALEARIC ISLANDS

PORTUGAL

M E S E T A

Tagus

• Toledo

VALENCIA

ESTREMADURA

Guadiana

CASTILE-LA MANCHA

Valencia •

Ibiza

3

Guadalquivir

MURCIA

Seville •

ANDALUSIA

Almonte •

Doñana
National
Park

Granada •

MEDITERRANEAN SEA

Málaga •

▲ Mulhacén
(11,411 feet/3,478 m)

Gibraltar (U.K.) •

4

Strait of Gibraltar

• Ceuta (Spain)

• Melilla (Spain)

ALGERIA

CANARY ISLANDS

Lanzarote

5

Tenerife

MOROCCO

▲ Pico de Teide
(12,198 ft /
3,718 m)

	International Boundary
	State Boundary
■	Capital
●	City
	River

42

Algeria D4
Almonte A4
Andalusia B3–B4
Andorra D2
Aragón C2
Asturias B1
Atlantic Ocean A2

Balearic Islands D3
Barcelona D2
Basque Country
    C1–C2
Bayonne C1
Bordeaux C1

Canary Islands A5
Cantabria B1
Cantabrian Mts. B2
Castile-La Mancha
    B3–C3
Castile-León B2
Catalonia D2
Ceuta B4
Costa Brava D2

Doñana National
    Park A4
Duero River B2

Ebro River C2
Estremadura A3–B3

Figueras D2
France D1

Galicia A1–A2
Gibraltar B4
Gijón B1
Granada B4
Guadalajara B2
Guadalquivir River
    B3

Above: The unique dragon tree (*right*) grows on the Canary Islands.

Guadiana River
    A3–B3
Guernica C1

Iberian Mountains
    C2
Ibiza D3

La Rioja C2
Lanzarote B5

Madrid B2
Málaga B4
Mediterranean Sea
    B4–D4
Melilla B4
Meseta B2–B3
Morocco B5
Mulhacén B4

Murcia C3

Navarra C2

Pico de Teide A5
Portugal A3
Pyrenees C2–D2

Salamanca B2
Saragossa C2

Seville B3
Strait of Gibraltar
    B4

Tagus River B3
Tenerife A5
Toledo B3

Valencia (city) C3
Valencia (region) C3

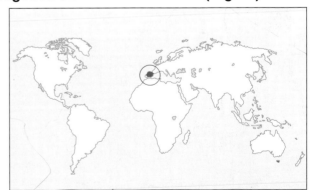

Quick Facts

Official Name   Kingdom of Spain

Capital   Madrid

Official Language   Castilian Spanish

Population   39.4 million

Land Area   194,898 square miles
(504,786 square kilometers)

Regions   Andalusia, Aragón, Asturias, Balearic Islands,
Basque Country, Canary Islands, Cantabria,
Castile-La Mancha, Castile-León, Catalonia,
Estremadura, Galicia, La Rioja, Madrid,
Murcia, Navarra, Valencia

Highest Point   On continental Spain: Pico de Mulhacén
(11,411 feet/3,478 m)

On Spanish territory: Pico de Teide on Tenerife
Island in the Canary Islands
(12,198 feet/3,718 m)

Major Rivers   Duero, Ebro, Guadalquivir, Guadiana, Tagus

Major Cities   Barcelona, Madrid, Málaga, Saragossa,
Seville, Valencia

Currency   Spanish Peseta (170 pesetas = U.S. $1 in 2000)

Opposite: Windmills are a common sight on Lanzarote Island.

44

Glossary

castanets: small instruments made up of two round shells of wood that are held in the hand and clicked together.

churros (CHEW-ros): sugary strips of fried dough.

coats of arms: specially designed symbols, usually in the form of a shield, that represent or identify specific groups, towns, or families.

communal: shared or participated in by an entire community.

cubist: a type of art in which objects are depicted as geometric shapes.

democracy: a system of government in which ultimate power rests with the people, who elect representatives.

fabada (fah-BAH-dah): a stew made from beans, sausage, and other meats.

ferias (feh-REE-uhs): popular fairs.

Gallego (guy-YAY-goh): the language spoken in Galicia; also known as Galician.

irrigation: supplying water to land by artificial means.

Lent: the period of forty days from Ash Wednesday to Easter, when Christians fast and show sorrow for their sins.

literate: able to read and write.

military dictatorship: a government in which the armed forces hold absolute power and authority.

Moors: the African Arabs and Berbers who ruled Spain from the eighth to the fifteenth century A.D.

New World: North and South America and the surrounding islands.

paella (pie-AY-yah): a rice dish with seafood or meat.

parliamentary monarchy: a system of government in which a monarch is the official head of state and of the armed forces. An elected prime minister, however, has the real power.

pilgrimages: journeys made by religious people to holy sites.

sangría (sang-GREE-ya): a drink made from red wine, fruit, and water.

siesta: an afternoon nap.

stabilized: became steady and secure.

tapas (TAH-pahs): Spanish appetizers or snacks.

vocational: related to a person's training or work in some kind of trade or profession.

More Books to Read

Celeste Sails to Spain. Alison Lester (Houghton Mifflin)

El Greco. Getting to Know the World's Greatest Artists series. Mike Venezia (Children's Press)

Los Pollitos Dicen/The Baby Chicks Sing. Nancy Abraham Hall and Jill Syverson-Stork (Little Brown & Co.)

Spain. Festivals of the World series. Susan McKay (Gareth Stevens)

Spain. Next Stop series. Clare Boast (Heineman Library)

Spain. Postcards from series. Helen Arnold (Raintree/Steck-Vaughn)

Spain: Picture a Country. Straightforward Science series. Henry Pluckrose (Franklin Watts)

Spanish Fairy Book. Gertrudis Segovia (Dover Publications)

The Three Golden Oranges. Alma Flor Ada (Atheneum)

Videos

Glory of Spain. (Video Artists International)

Spain. (IVN Entertainment)

Spain: Costa Brava. (Education 2000)

Spain: Toledo, Madrid, Seville, and Andalusia. (Questar Inc.)

Web Sites

www.red2000.com/Spain/index.html

www.odci.gov/cia/publications/ factbook/sp.html

www.tardis.ed.ac.uk/~angus/Gallery/ Photos/Europe/Spain/index.html

www.ozemail.com.au/~spain/cooking.htm

Due to the dynamic nature of the Internet, some web sites stay current longer than others. To find additional web sites about Spain, use a reliable search engine and enter one or more of the following keywords: *Barcelona, bullfighting, Christopher Columbus, flamenco, Isabella I, Madrid, Moors, paella, Picasso, Spain.*

Index